INK COURAGE ™

31 DAYS
OF
ENCOURAGEMENT

Daily Quotes & Pep-Talks to
Empower the Shit Out of You!

Warning: Light profanity and heavy female empowerment

You were meant to have this for a reason.
If you're going through a tough time, or just need
a little extra push, this book is for you. You have
the strength, the wit, the potential, the passion,
the heart and everything in between to accomplish
whatever you want in life. Inkcourage believes in
you and is here to help you follow your dreams.

GIRL, GET THIS FREE WORKBOOK!

Download at:

www.inkcourage.org/31DaysofEncouragement

Questions to follow along with each day!

SOO...WHAT'S INKCOURAGE?

We're Inkcourage! We encourage through ink *(get it?)*. We design and sell encouraging temporary tattoos, apparel and more so that others can physically wear encouraging words wherever they go. Our main mission is to be a vehicle for others to encourage and be encouraged. We believe in intersectional feminism, empowering not only women, but people of all cultures, genders, and identities.

With this book, we hope that you'll not only be empowered to go and take on the world, but that you empower others around you every single day. We hope that you're so inspired that you'll rip out the pages and send them to a friend, read the pages more than once, read them in order and out of order, and even pass the book on to someone who needs it. Encouragement can truly make us invincible.

Keep encouraging!

- Ange
FOUNDER OF INKCOURAGE

YOU ARE EXACTLY WHERE YOU NEED TO BE.

To start, we need to get this straight... realize you are meant to be here in this moment. You are at the right place in your life, your career, your family, and your goals at this point in time. You are exactly where you need to be. You are not falling behind, you are not too old, you are not incapable. You are exactly where you need to be... not where anyone else expects you to be, not where you think you should be "at this age." We've seen so many people compare themselves to others their same age, but everyone works at their own pace. Everyone is on their own path. You are meant to be here in this moment—Let's make the most of it.

WHERE DO YOU THINK YOU "SHOULD BE?"

OK, now, take a moment to completely disregard what you just said as being true. We think you need to hear this from yourself...
WHY IS YOUR ANSWER TO THE PREVIOUS QUESTION A LIE?

Great, now that that's out of the way, you can open your heart up to some real encouragement.

YOU LIVE MOST OF YOUR LIFE INSIDE OF YOUR HEAD, MAKE IT A NICE PLACE TO BE.

2

We are our own worst enemy. We're constantly telling ourselves we're not good enough, not strong enough, not beautiful enough. Sometimes, we honestly believe we don't deserve the best things in life. The more we think these negative thoughts, the more we believe them. So, you know what?! Let's just not think this way any longer. These negative thoughts are not true. We repeat, NOT TRUE. You are good enough, you are strong enough, you are beautiful enough, and you are capable of achieving anything and everything you want. Let's make our heads a nice place to be by filling them with positive thoughts. Now, encouragement isn't a one-time thing. It is a process. You may feel inspired now, but if you want to be forever changed, you need to tackle this head-on every single day. Think of yourself as a fucking goddess warrior princess. Every single time you have a negative thought about yourself, fucking slash that thing down with your laser beams (or whatever it is you do to get rid of things you don't want). Don't believe the negative thoughts you tell yourself. You're the shit — Never forget it, not for a single second.

So, how can we overcome our currently negative perceptions? Let's start with positive self-talk.

GIVE YOURSELF THREE REASONS WHY YOU'RE AN ABSOLUTE BADASS.

1.

2.

3.

Yup, we completely agree with all of those. Now, on a sticky note or other piece of paper, write a positive affirmation. Post it in your room or on your bathroom mirror, somewhere you'll see it every day.

WHAT'S YOUR POSITIVE AFFIRMATION? WHAT DO YOU NEED TO HEAR EVERY SINGLE DAY TO HELP YOURSELF OVERCOME SELF-DOUBT AND NEGATIVE SELF-TALK?

DREAM BIG ASS DREAMS

3 Sometimes when we stop believing in ourselves and our abilities, we think our dreams are out of reach. However, now that you know you're capable of anything, we can start dreaming again. Any successful people you see have gone through hardships. The reason they're still successful is because no matter what has happened to them, they've never stopped dreaming. Steve Jobs was fired from Apple. He then made his own competing company, was rehired by Apple, and is now known to be one of the biggest dreamers who ever existed. Oprah grew up in poverty. She eventually became a news reporter before being fired and told she'd never make it in television (spoiler alert: we all know Oprah is one of the most successful people in the world). If Oprah or Steve Jobs just accepted the opinions of others and believed they weren't good enough, our lives and the world as we know it would be completely different. Of course, these two people are extremely famous. You might be thinking, "I'm never going to be that successful." Oprah and Steve might have thought the exact same thing before they made it big. If you're going to dream, don't minimize the possibilities. If you're going to be a _____ , be the best damn _____ you can be. Dream Oprah-sized dreams.

NOW THAT YOU CAN DO ANYTHING, WHAT WILL YOU DO?
- BRUCE MAU

Let's take some time to dream.
WHAT ARE YOU PASSIONATE ABOUT?

WHAT DO YOU WANT TO ACCOMPLISH IN LIFE? AT THE VERY LEAST, WHO DO YOU WANT TO BE?

SO, WHY ARE YOU THE BEST PERSON FOR THIS? (Don't give any BS, you are the best person to do exactly this. Start believing in yourself RIGHT NOW!)

DREAM BIG,
START SMALL,
BUT MOST OF ALL,
START.

-SIMON SINEK-

4

What have you always wanted to do? What have you always wanted to be? Yes, think of that thing that has been rattling in your head for years. If you've been thinking about it for this long, don't think of it any longer. Make it happen. Start small. Think of one small step you can take to make your dreams happen. What is the first move? If you have an idea for a small business, maybe start with your vision. What do you want this business to look like? What will you sell? Maybe you want to redo your bathroom. Start making a list of everything you want to get done or change. Maybe you want to move out of your parents' house, or maybe you want to move back home and save money because that's 100% valid and honestly undervalued. Get a budgeting app on your phone and start keeping track of your money, limit yourself when you want to spend $300 at Target. Whatever it is, put your ideas on paper and start to make your dreams a reality. After you take your first step, the second one doesn't seem so scary.

WHAT DREAM WILL YOU PUT INTO ACTION?

WHAT'S YOUR FIRST STEP?

SHOOT
YOUR
SHOT.

5

We're often stuck between choices and directions, and it's a gamble to decide what to do next. When you're afraid to take a risk, ask yourself, "What's the worst that can happen?" If you're making a business decision, maybe the worst outcome would be losing money. If that's the end of the world for you, don't risk it. If you feel you're in the right place to take a hit, then take the risk (shit happens). However, if you always choose to play it safe, you'll never know and you'll never grow. When making a potentially risky decision, think about it like this: "*If I don't take this chance, will I always wonder, 'what if?'*" Once you're no longer afraid of the reasons why you shouldn't do something, think of the reasons why you should do it. What's the best that can happen? How could your life dramatically change for the better? Why is it sooo worth it to take this risk? Let your purpose be stronger than your fears. The risk is worth the reward. Shoot your shot.

WHAT SHOT ARE YOU TRYNA' SHOOT?

WHAT'S THE WORST THAT CAN HAPPEN?

WHAT'S THE BEST THAT CAN HAPPEN?

TRUST YOUR PATH

Oh hey, did we mention there isn't just one path for you? If you choose Door Number One, it doesn't mean Door Number Two is closed forever. It might feel like your options are limited, but there are so many opportunities out there you don't even realize. New doors are being created as we speak. Want some encouraging facts? The crazy thing is that the world will completely change in the next ten years. There's a study done by the *Institute for the Future* that says "85% of jobs in the 2030s aren't created yet." In the near future, jobs will be completely different, and even society's judgments and expectations will change in ways we can't even imagine. Don't believe us? Look back to the past ten years and see how far we've come. We no longer take digital cameras on vacation, we use our phones. We get in strangers' cars and sleep in strangers' houses via Uber and Airbnb. We even watch ordinary people become millionaires for playing video games or showing us their skincare routine. The possibilities in life are so endless, our present-day brains can't even fathom it. Your future is so fucking bright. You're gonna be just fine.

HOW IS YOUR LIFE DIFFERENT THAN IT WAS TEN YEARS AGO?

There isn't one path for you. Don't limit yourself to the path you think you need to be on. Let's go bigger.

WHAT ARE THREE FUTURE PATHS YOU SEE FOR YOURSELF?

1.

2.

3.

FUCK FEAR

7

Fear is often the biggest obstacle between people and their dreams. Sometimes we know our fears are completely irrational, yet they have a clutch on our lives and everything we do. Take cats for instance - they have this natural instinct to be afraid of cucumbers (if you haven't seen this, google it now). Of course, when we see cats being afraid of cucumbers, it seems irrational. When a cat is afraid of a cucumber, we can call that cat out and say "you're being dramatic, calm down, it's just a cucumber." But when we're afraid of irrational things, we let those fears completely take over our minds to the point that we can't even get out of bed. Sometimes our friends call us out and say, "you're being dramatic, calm down, it's just a cucumber," but it's hard for us to actually believe this. The fear and anxiety is still there. Worry will always be inside of us. So, we have a choice to either let our fears consume us or to move regardless of them and become courageous. Do it afraid.

Call out your "cucumber" fears one by one, and let's conquer them.

WHAT ARE YOUR THREE BIGGEST FEARS RIGHT NOW?

LET'S KNOCK THEM DOWN. WHY ARE THEY JUST "CUCUMBERS?" HOW CAN YOU OVERCOME THEM?

WHAT WOULD HAPPEN IF YOU WERE YOUR BEST, STRONG, AND COURAGEOUS SELF? HOW WOULD YOU LIVE DIFFERENTLY EVERY DAY?

DO WHAT YOU LOVE!

8

Let's aim to live our best lives and do what we love! Though an overused phrase that has lost much of its value, "life is too short" is the exact motto we should live by. You only have one life; do you want to spend it doing what you love or wondering what your life could've been like if you did? Yes, this sounds really harsh for an encouragement book, but we're honestly here to tell you the cold hard truth. Imagine if you lived your life doing what you love every single day. Maybe for you this means completely changing your career, or maybe you love your job but you want to make new friends. Maybe you want to travel the world or learn how to salsa dance. Think about what would make YOU happier. If you did what you love every day, how would you feel? How would you act? Would you treat life differently? Would you treat your family and friends differently? You're not selfish or foolish for wanting to do what you love. If you could be happier, live happier, and feel more fulfilled, you need to start taking action. Like, right now. So, are you ready or not?

Think about what would make YOU happier.
HOW WOULD YOU FEEL? HOW WOULD YOU ACT? WOULD YOU TREAT LIFE
DIFFERENTLY? WOULD YOU TREAT YOUR FAMILY AND FRIENDS DIFFERENTLY?

JUST BECAUSE IT DIDN'T HAPPEN OVERNIGHT,
DOESN'T MEAN IT WON'T EVER HAPPEN.

GOOD THINGS TAKE TIME.

9

Sometimes the cheesy phrases your grandmother always said are actually true. Our culture today thrives on "instant gratification," and honestly, we blame microwaves. Microwaves allowed us to believe we can have a seven-course meal in two minutes or less, and they were right *(shout out to those Kid Cuisines)*. Let's be honest, if a Lyft ride takes more than ten minutes, it's the most frustrating thing in the world. We're not saying everyone lives in the mindset of instant gratification, but it's good to know the type of person you are. Next time you're "waiting," notice your patterns. Do you get stressed out? Are you completely fine with waiting? Maybe for certain things you're completely fine waiting, and for others, you're not. For example, maybe you're fine waiting in line for groceries, but you're not down waiting for the perfect job. When you're frustrated because you can't find the right job (or whatever it is), is it because you want a job now? Or is it because you're worried you'll never find one? Good things take serious time. Put in the time and the work. Things might not happen overnight, but that doesn't mean they'll never happen. While you're waiting, enjoy the ride.

WHAT HAVE YOU BEEN WAITING ON?

Good things take time.
HOW CAN YOU MAKE THE MOST OF YOUR "WAITING"?

FEEL WHAT YOU
NEED TO FEEL & THEN
LET IT GO.

DO NOT LET IT CONSUME YOU.

—DHIMAN

10

Life is always going to deal you bad cards and shitty roadblocks. It's OK to be mad at the crappy hand, just don't let it destroy you.

First, we should say depression is a real thing. Anxiety is a real thing.
We don't want to discredit issues regarding mental health. But, your mental health will absolutely decline when you feel like nothing can help and nothing will change.

People can help. You can be happy. You deserve happiness. We can make small changes in our lives to be happier every single day. If you seriously don't want to get out of bed to go to school, treat yourself to Starbucks every time you do. If you struggle with people at work, think of reasons why they're amazing and brilliant, and choose not to get annoyed with them every time they do something you hate. Move out of discomfort and out of general unhappiness. Make choices that will benefit your mindset. Choose to be happy.

WHAT ASPECTS OF YOUR LIFE ARE YOU CURRENTLY UNHAPPY WITH?

SO, WHAT MAKES YOU HAPPY?

HOW CAN YOU CHOOSE TO BE HAPPIER IN YOUR CURRENT SITUATION AND EACH DAY MOVING FORWARD?

If you feel like you are depressed or have anxiety, talk to someone. Talk to a professional, hire a therapist, or call the suicide hot-line number. 1-800-273-8255.

THE BIGGEST
MIS/TAKE YOU
CAN MAKE
                    TOO
IS BEING ^ AFRAID
TO MAKE ONE!

11

Failure is a really hard pill to swallow. We grew up in a system that rewarded success and gave punishment for failure. This mindset made us ashamed to fail and it made us afraid to even try. Society gives participation awards so that kids don't feel crappy for losing. There's a stigma that losing is a bad thing and it starts at an early age. If losing didn't matter, why the hell does everyone get a trophy? Odds are, you will fail thousands of times in your life. Failure is inevitable. Since you know you'll fail, you can change your perspective on it before it even happens. You can either respond or react. You can let your failure consume you, constantly second-guessing your abilities and your path. Or, you can let failure fuel you, by taking each moment as a new opportunity to learn and grow. Don't let your failures tell a negative story of who you are. Your failure does not define your worth or your value. Keep failing and become stronger every single time.

WHEN'S THE LAST TIME YOU "FAILED"? HOW DID YOU FEEL?

Now, switch your mindset. Failure is a part of life.
WHAT WOULD YOU TELL SOMEONE WHO WAS IN YOUR SITUATION?
WHAT PEP TALK WOULD YOU GIVE?

Next time you "fail" or are afraid of failing, read your statement ^. Take your own advice ;).

YOU ALREADY HAVE WHAT IT TAKES!

12

Yup, YOU. You have so much power you don't even understand!!!! You alone have the ability to do and be whatever you want. Do you want to save the sea turtles? Save those little guys. Do you want to end global warming? End that shit. Do you want to lift a car with your bare hands? More power to you. The crazy thing is, each and every one of us is so powerful, we either forget it or just don't see it inside of us.

Greta Thunberg is one of the faces of climate change. Greta is 16 years old, from Sweden and was born with Asperger's. No one would ever think a teen-ager with Asperger's would be at the forefront of climate change, but she is. The crazy thing is, even when she's doing something good and positive in this world, people are throwing her shade. When you're on top of your game and absolutely killing it at life, there will be people who try to bring you down and tell you that you can't do something. Don't doubt your power. Greta is not going to stop and neither should you. You are so strong, powerful and capable. You can fucking do anything you set your mind to.

WHAT WILL YOU DO WITH YOUR POWER?

YOU CAN HAVE
A KIND HEART
& STILL SAY NO.

13

Self-care seems like the theme of the decade. In life, we've been told that self-care is selfish behavior. When your friends ask you to go out, you should always say yes, right? When your family asks you for a favor, you should legit drop everything you're doing and come through.

You know yourself better than anyone else in this world. If you're working crazy hours and coming home exhausted, you're allowed to take the night to re-energize yourself. If you haven't had a free weekend in a while, and your great-aunt asks you to watch her dog, you're allowed to say no. If you're afraid of what your friends or family will think, just be straight up with them right off the bat. (Even though it's tempting to say "maybe" and let them down easy via text, you can save yourself that unneeded pain for the next four weeks dreading finally saying "no"…). Be honest with yourself and others, and say no when you want to say no. Your mental health matters. If they care about you, they'll understand.

WHAT ARE THE TOP THREE MOST STRESSFUL THINGS YOU'RE DEALING WITH RIGHT NOW?

HOW CAN YOU INTERVENE THIS WEEK AND PRACTICE SELF-CARE IN THESE SITUATIONS?

IT'S OK TO NOT BE OK.

14

For years, we have bared the burden of so many things. We've been told to suck it up and put on a brave face. Hey, it's OK to not be OK. We are human. We have emotions, we have struggles, we have hardships. It's not good to bottle it up and push through. Let it all out, have a good cry, talk to a friend, talk to a therapist, eat a pint of Ben & Jerry's— whatever you've got to do! We encourage you to talk about your problems, but we know it can be hard. If it's too hard to talk to someone, first, talk to yourself. Write it down in a journal and let it all out on paper. When the time is right and you're ready, you can talk to someone. Know that you have people in your corner rooting for you, and people who want to help you get through it. Don't worry about "burdening" your friends with your problems. We weren't meant to do life alone. Friends and family are there to help you through the hard times. You are brave and can make it through anything. Someone believes in you.

NEVERTHELESS,
YOU PERSISTED.

So many amazing people have gone through depression, bullying, stress, anxiety, cancer, and disease. Life sucks, and no one should have to go through any of this. All across the world, people have gone through struggles but you know what else they all have? The strength to keep fighting. They kept going even when the world was stacked against them. You might be going through something serious, and your whole life could have been a struggle, but you will make it through. Each and every human was made with this insane resilience to shine through the darkest moments. You have insane potential. You are strong as hell. You will get through this. Never stop persisting.

15

WHAT CURRENT BATTLE ARE YOU GOING THROUGH?

WHAT DOUBTS OR FEARS DO YOU HAVE?

Right now, write an affirmation to yourself.
WHY WILL YOU GET THROUGH THIS?

GET
SHIT
DONE ✓

16

Yass, let's slay the fucking day. Got a lot of shit to do? Get your ass in gear and let's start doing it. You know those moments when you somehow bend time and space and get everything done with five seconds to spare? Yes, girl. This is one of those moments. When google maps tells you you'll get there in 30 minutes, you get there in 28. When your paper is due at midnight, you finish at 11:59 and it's some of your best work. When you're out of food, you channel your inner Rachel fucking Ray, make some random shit, and it turns out dope. You are killing it every single day. You are a savage and are capable of whatever you put your mind to. You've got this, and you already know. Let's fucking go. Let's get shit done.

GIRL, HOW CAN YOU MAXIMIZE YOUR TIME AND GET SHIT DONE?

OK, now *get to work!*

DON'T BELIEVE THE HATERS

The haters are always gonna hate. They might be jealous or they might be bored, who the hell knows! But frankly, it doesn't really matter, does it? Yes, it can be so tempting to clap back at the haters, but you're bigger than that. You really don't need those haters in your life. You know your true self and your true intentions! Instead of getting mad at the people bringing you down, remind yourself of your truth. You know yourself better than your doubters. Don't believe the haters, believe in yourself.

Let's officially forget the haters by taking this self-proclaimed oath.

Oath to the haters:

TO ALL THE HATERS WHO HAVE HATED BEFORE,

I _____, DO NOT AND WILL NOT BELIEVE THE HATERS. EVEN WHEN THE HATERS
     YOUR NAME

_____ AND _____, I WILL _____ _____ _____ . I WILL STAND TALL
    VERB   VERB   BLANK   BLANK   BLANK

BECAUSE I AM A _____, _____ _____ . I WILL NOT BELIEVE THE HATERS. I WILL
               ADJECTIVE   ADJECTIVE   NOUN

BELIEVE MYSELF.

REMEMBER WHY YOU STARTED.

18

When you're overworked, and tired AF, the struggle becomes real. When you're so completely drained, you don't even realize three weeks have passed by until you have no food in your fridge and you ran out of clean socks. Somehow in these moments of stress, there just aren't enough hours in the day to get everything done. The struggle is at an absolute peak. This stress becomes the focus in our lives, and we forget why we're putting ourselves through the stress in the first place. Maybe you're going to school and exams and essays are killing you. Remember why you wanted to pursue your major or an education in the first place. Maybe your kids won't stop nagging you and are draining every ounce of your energy. Remember why you love your kids and how you first felt when they arrived in the world; somehow seeing the positive in people (including your own children) can flip your mindset. Let your purpose fuel your fire and help it keep you going. Remember why you started and don't forget it.

WHAT CURRENT <u>STRUGGLE</u> ARE YOU GOING THROUGH NOW?

WHAT ABOUT (<u>REASON ABOVE</u>) MADE YOU WANT TO START IT IN THE FIRST PLACE?

YOU HAVE THE SAME HOURS IN A DAY AS BEYONCÉ*

* EXCEPT YOUR DAY IS NOTHING LIKE BEYONCÉ'S BECAUSE SHE HAS MILLIONS OF DOLLARS AND A TEAM FULL OF PEOPLE. DON'T COMPARE YOUR WORK ETHIC. YOU'RE DOING JUST FINE.

19

It's a myth to think, "If I'm not successful, I'm not working hard enough." This is the hustlers' mentality and this is a lie. You can work so hard every single day and feel like you're going nowhere. Yes, you should absolutely work hard, but we want to change the stigma of hard work. Millennials have a bad rep for being lazy and not working hard enough. Sometimes, they get advice like, *"You need to put in the extra hours and it will pay off"* or *"Oh, maybe you're not trying hard enough."* Working harder might pay off, but don't work harder to prove that you're a hard worker. Don't burn yourself out just because Karen from accounting doesn't see you busting your ass. You yourself aren't valuable because you can pull an all-nighter or a double shift. Your work ethic is between you and only you. You know how hard you work and what you bring to the table. Be confident in that. You have nothing to prove.

Write down a reminder for yourself. WHY ARE *YOU* KILLIN' IT, DOIN' WHAT YOU'RE DOIN', EVERY SINGLE DAY?

MAKE BOLD MOVES

20

Have you ever walked into an art museum and thought, *"This is art? I can paint that."* Yes, you probably can...but, did you? (No.) Will you? (Ehh..) When was the last time you painted ... elementary school? (Maybe.) It's so much easier to say you can do something than actually doing it. We've all had moments like this where we've seen people do things that we're totally capable of doing ourselves. The difference between them and you is that they took action. They made moves. So many people are unhappy with their current situation in life and yet do nothing about it. A lot of people are constantly miserable with their job and to have yet to make a change. Some people want to start a business and have been sitting on their ideas for years. You don't have to do something huge to do something worthwhile. Take action on the things that matter most to you. If your work culture sucks, come up with some solutions. If you saw something awesome on Pinterest, go to a craft store and start working. Make moves. Be the type of person who not only sees that painting and says, *"Oh damn, I can do that."* Be the type of person who sees the painting then goes out and gets shit done.

WHAT WILL IT TAKE FOR YOU TO TAKE ACTION ON YOUR GOALS AND DREAMS?

IT DOES NOT MATTER
HOW FAST YOU GO,
AS LONG AS YOU
DO NOT STOP.

→ → →

21

If you're tired, exhausted, and just flat out done, don't quit, just take baby steps. You might quit because you're not winning or you're not successful. You might quit because you're exhausted and just tired of trying. You might quit because you feel like nothing can and will change. Don't define your value by where you're at in the race, know your value and know that you can do better. If the Wright Brothers quit after their first prototype didn't take flight, they would have never built a successful plane. The crazy thing is, the Wright Brothers worked for four years before any of their planes actually took flight, FOUR YEARS (Oh, and the Wright Brothers were high school dropouts)! Oh, and their first "flight" was only 12 seconds long. After year three, they could have been like, *"naw, brah, this is never gonna happen"*, buttt they didn't stop and now they're in the frickin' Smithsonian. If you stop now, how will you know how far you can go?

Don't stop. Keep going.

WHAT'S A SITUATION THAT YOU'VE BEEN THINKING ABOUT "QUITTING"?
WHY DO YOU WANT TO QUIT?

SEE YOUR SITUATION DIFFERENTLY. INSTEAD OF QUITTING, HOW CAN YOU
PUSH YOURSELF TO KEEP MOVING?

CHANGE BEGINS AT THE EDGE OF YOUR COMFORT ZONE

Have you found yourself stuck in your routine? Have you gotten used to the day to day? When's the last time you did something out of your comfort zone? When's the last time you did something crazy? If you're waiting for a sign, this is it. Be the best version of yourself every damn day (only you really know what that is, and if you're not achieving that.) Of course, sometimes when there's no one pushing us, or we're locked in this really comfortable job, there isn't any incentive to get better or do better. Yeah, it's really great to get home at a reasonable time and be able to watch a few shows on Netflix. But, after you've finished watching The Office for the fourth time, are you ever wondering, what's next? Discover what's beyond. Change begins at the end of your comfort zone.

WHAT CURRENT STRUGGLE ARE YOU GOING THROUGH NOW?

WHAT ABOUT (REASON ABOVE) MADE YOU WANT TO START IT IN THE FIRST PLACE?

NEVER STOP
LEARNING.

23

When's the last time you were bad at something? Like, truly bad. Like, your friends almost disowned you, bad? Maybe you were completely frustrated and quit right then and there, or maybe you laughed your ass off at how horrible you were. Either way, you tried something completely new. Congrats! Somehow, after the age of ten, it can feel so embarrassing and stupid that you don't know everything that exists in the world. There are only so many hours in the day, there's no way that you can know everythinggg. Let's change our mindset. Instead of feeling horrible for not know-ing the right answers, let's ask more questions. What's so wrong about not knowing? Let's change the mindset that we're not igno-rant, we're just not yet informed. :) If we're afraid to ask or afraid to do something, we're never going to grow and we're never going to learn. We should always be learning, even when we're 99.

WHAT'S SOMETHING NEW YOU WANT TO LEARN? WHAT'S SOME-THING NEW YOU WANT TO DO?

LIVE IN THE MOMENT

24

Life moves so freaking fast and it can be easy to let the moment slip away. Mindfulness is a huge trend because it allows us to be more present and become way more aware. A common misconception is that young adults are too focused on themselves or their phones to "live in the moment." We're in this crazy period of time where we have the ability to access the world from our phone. We have a lot we're doing, and honestly, technology helps us do it (*sorry for evolving the human race.*) Those millennials that are "*attached to their phones*" might be doing some important shit. On your phone alone, you can order groceries, book a flight, track your friends, run a business, buy a car or phone a friend in any country in the world (*Msg & data rates may apply*). Technology allows us to work and be active every single minute of the day. Although technology is a tool, sometimes being so accessible to it can overwork us. You deserve to disconnect and not work every minute just because you can. Living in the moment can **literally** be sitting in your car with your eyes closed and thinking of all of the things you're thankful for. Or, you can take a moment, download a podcast and do a few breathing exercises before work. When you're going a million miles a minute, don't forget to take time for yourself and live in your moment. You deserve every moment this world has to offer.

HOW CAN YOU SLOW YOUR LIFE DOWN AND LIVE IN THE MOMENT?

YOU'RE A FUCKING BADASS

You are so completely insanely gifted in every way. Your unique talents and strengths radiate from every inch of you. Don't dull your sparkle. You are not inferior and should not feel inferior to anyone else around you. Encouragement makes us invincible and reminds us of the true badass we are every single day. When you feel like yourself and feel so fucking great, don't you believe you can do anything? You are a badass. You wake up every single day and make the most of what you have. Don't doubt yourself or your own abilities. You are a badass no matter who you are. The best part is, your badassery is uniquely you. Even if you're a hard-ass and think you have no value- think of how you can use your strengths for good. If you're a hard-ass, you can get others to stick to goals, you're tough on your friends when they're being stupid and you don't take any B.S. You're goofy? You can make people laugh in awkward situations and break the ice in tense moments. The best things about you— your personality— is unique to you. Our motivations can accomplish insane things. Be the badass your five-year-old self knew you were.

WHAT MAKES YOU A BADASS?

TOUGH TO SAY? WHEN INTERVIEWERS ASK YOU, "HOW WOULD YOUR FRIENDS DESCRIBE YOU?" WHAT WOULD YOU SAY?

I WILL NOT COMPARE MYSELF TO A STRANGER ON INSTAGRAM

First of all, we want to say that no one has it all together, even if their Instagram says otherwise. Remember that celebrities have trainers, diet coaches, tweaking apps and everything to make them look their best. It's literally their job to make you in awe of them and make you the ultimate Stan. So, you might be thinking, well what about the people you know? Most people put their best face forward on Instagram, even if they're not celebs.

Second, you don't need to compare yourself to others. We have been unconsciously taught from a young age if we're not thin enough or pretty enough, we aren't valuable. That it an unhealthy way of thinking. Of course, you can always strive to be healthier and put yourself out there, but don't make changes because of a societal standard. We need to not just accept ourselves as we are, but LOVE ourselves and be confident in who we are.

"IT WAS WHEN I REALIZED I NEEDED TO STOP TRYING TO BE SOMEBODY ELSE AND BE MYSELF, THAT I ACTUALLY STARTED TO OWN, ACCEPT AND LOVE WHAT I HAD."
TRACEE ELLIS ROSS

WHAT UNHEALTHY STANDARDS HAVE YOU BEEN COMPARING YOURSELF TO?
(Also, this doesn't have to be outside features, it can be money, social status or anything that makes you compare).

WHAT WILL IT TAKE FOR YOU TO STOP COMPARING YOURSELF TO OTHERS AND START ACCEPTING YOURSELF?

ENCOURAGEMENT IS CONTAGIOUS!

27

Now that you have a taste of encouragement, this is your moment to go out and encourage others. These last five days will be focused on how you have the power to encourage others. Maybe that means ripping a page out of this book and giving it to a friend (our hope is that you actually give this whole book to a friend or a stranger after and spread the encouragement). You have the power and ability to make some serious changes just with your words alone. Words have this crazy ability to either tear us down or build us up. Think back in your life. You probably remember both something negative and positive someone told you as a kid. Words are powerful. Words stick with us and completely affect our lives. You have the power to spread positivity or negativity with your words alone. Know the power of your words, and know that you can make a positive lasting impact on someone's life.

Encouragement is contagious—Go spread it.

HAS SOMEONE'S WORDS STUCK WITH YOU?
HOW DID THESE WORDS MAKE YOU FEEL?

Now, you have the power.
HOW CAN YOU ENCOURAGE OTHERS EVERY SINGLE DAY?

IF YOU SEE SOMETHING GOOD IN SOMEONE, SPEAK IT.

28

For some crazy reason, even when we have nice things to say about people, we don't always say it. Maybe we're afraid of what they think, maybe it's an awkward relationship, or maybe you don't want to feed into their ego. Let's live life with an open encouragement filter and speak the positive things we see in people. If you love someone's bright green hair, tell them. If you saw someone do something kind for a stranger, let them know it didn't go unnoticed. Being kind can seriously change someone's whole day, year and life. Have you ever just said hi to someone and their whole face lit up? Have you ever complimented someone and their mood instantly changed? Someone could be having the shittiest day or week or year and that can make a huge difference. Also, sometimes, kindness isn't appreciated, but don't let that kill your vibe. Again, we all know you might never know what someone is going through. If you have positive things to say, say them.

WHAT GOOD THINGS HAVE YOU NOTICED IN YOUR FAMILY, YOUR FRIENDS, AND YOUR COLLEAGUES LATELY?

HAVE YOU TOLD THEM YOU APPRECIATE ALL OF THESE AMAZING QUALITIES?
If not, take a moment to write an appreciation text and let them know all of the amazing things you're thinking. You have the power to change their mood just through these texts.

BE THE FRIEND
YOU WISH TO SEE
IN YOUR DMS

29

How many times have you heard, "my friends never text me" or " my friends never ask to hang out" or "I haven't heard from them, they're probably mad at me". Well, Becky, when's the last time that you called your friends? Do you ask them to hang out? Do you ask them deep questions about their life? If you do, awesome! Keep doing that. If you don't, you're the answer to your problems. Make it the norm to reach out to your friends and ask them about their day. Ask them to hang out and actually dig deep and find out what's going on in their life. It's a known fact about life, if you want friends who are invested in your life, you need to start investing in your friends' lives. People want to be around people who care. Odds are, your friends could be going through something big and you'd have no idea. Even Meghan Markle admitted that not enough people are checking in on her! If Meghan Markle needs a DM, we all do. We know you probably do care about your friends, but don't forget to show them you care. Make that extra special effort and you'll see dramatic changes in each one of your friendships. Give a damn about your friends and they'll give a damn about you.

WHAT ARE SOME WAYS YOU CAN BE THE BEST FRIEND YOU CAN BE?

WHAT RELATIONSHIPS DO YOU WANT TO BUILD? WHO DO YOU WANT TO REACH OUT TO?

DON'T BE JEALOUS, CELEBRATE!

30

As kids, we always fought over toys with friends and had to learn how to share. Instead of being so happy that our friend got the best toy in the world, we were mad because we wanted that same exact toy. Or, maybe you were the kid who was jealous when it was someone else's birthday. They got to blow out all the candles, eat the first piece of cake and open all of the presents (and you secretly wanted the gift you got them.) Even when we were celebrating, we were still jealous. Still sounds familiar? The next time someone has good news, celebrate it. Ask them about it. Appreciate it as if it's your own. You'd be surprised by how many times we internally don't celebrate because of how we feel. The world isn't about us. Encouragement is contagious, and so is joy. When someone wins, we all win. If we have the ability to make others feel good, why wouldn't we?

Celebrate. Life is so much more fun when you do.

Let's think of some of your friends, family, and coworkers!
HOW CAN YOU CELEBRATE WHAT THEY'RE DOING THIS WEEK?

CHOOSE KINDNESS

31

Kindness is so magical that it has the ability to instantly change worlds around us. Choose Kindness. Yup. We said choose. Kindness is a choice. When Ellen DeGeneres sat next to President Bush at a football game, the whole country went wild. People wondered, *"How can they laugh together when they stand for completely different things*?" Ellen boiled it down to one thing, kindness. *"When I say, 'be kind to one another,' I don't only mean the people that think the same way that you do. I mean be kind to everyone."* We all have our differences, and it's OK to disagree. Disagreements don't give us permission to treat people like they're not human. There is no one in this world that is more valuable than anyone else. We all deserve compassion, and compassion doesn't cost a damn thing. Kindness is magic, don't underestimate it.

INK COURAGE ™

I hope you finished this book feeling a little more encouraged than when you started! You are insanely gifted in your own unique way, and have the power to affect some serious change in this world.

What's next?

Pass this book on to a friend who needs it most – rip out a few pages and even frame them in your house. You have the power to encourage those around you.

Want to keep encouraging? Check out our website www.inkcourage.org and see our encouraging temporary tattoos, stickers, apparel and more! Encourage yourself, encourage and friend - the world will be a better place. Encouragement is contagious!

Keep encouraging,

- Ange

FOUNDER OF INKCOURAGE

FEEL ENCOURAGED?

Review this book on Amazon and let us know!

bit.ly/31DaysAmazon